AARDVARKS

Maddie Gibbs

PowerKiDS press™
New York

For my mom and other garnfark appreciators

Published in 2011 by The Rosen Publishing Group, Inc.
29 East 21st Street, New York, NY 10010

First Edition

Editor: Amelie von Zumbusch
Layout Design: Greg Tucker

Photo Credits: Cover Berndt Fischer/Getty Images; p. 5 Joel Sartore/Getty Images; pp. 7, 15, 20–21 Nigel Dennis/Getty Images; pp. 9, 24 (bottom left) Doug Cheeseman/Peter Arnold, Inc.; pp. 11, 24 (top right) © Nigel Dennis/age fotostock; pp. 13, 24 (top left) Alan Root/Getty Images; pp. 17, 24 (bottom right) © Alan Root/ Peter Arnold, Inc.; p. 19 Anthony Bannister/Getty Images; pp. 22–23 © APA/ Peter Arnold, Inc.

Library of Congress Cataloging-in-Publication Data

Gibbs, Maddie.
 Aardvarks / by Maddie Gibbs. — 1st ed.
     p. cm. — (Safari animals)
 Includes index.
 ISBN 978-1-4488-3187-6 (library binding) — ISBN 978-1-4488-3188-3 (pbk.) — ISBN 978-1-4488-3189-0 (6-pack)
 1. Aardvark—Juvenile literature. I. Title.
 QL737.T8G53 2011
 599.3'1—dc22

                          2010025811

Manufactured in the United States of America

CPSIA Compliance Information: Batch #WW11PK: For Further Information contact Rosen Publishing, New York, New York at 1-800-237-9932

Contents

This strange-looking animal
is an aardvark.

5

Aardvarks live in Africa. They can be found in both forests and grasslands.

Aardvarks have long **snouts**.
They have big ears, too.

9

Aardvarks have sharp **claws**. Their claws make them very good at digging.

11

Aardvarks dig **burrows**. They most often sleep in their burrows during the day.

13

In the evening, aardvarks leave their burrows to look for food.

15

Aardvarks often break open **termite mounds** to suck out the termites.

17

Aardvarks dig up ants, too. They eat around 50,000 insects each night!

19

Most of the time, aardvarks live by themselves.

21

However, baby aardvarks live with their mothers.

23

Words to Know

burrow

claw

snout

termite mound

Index

Web Sites

Due to the changing nature of Internet links, PowerKids Press has developed an online list of Web sites related to the subject of this book. This site is updated regularly. Please use this link to access the list:
www.powerkidslinks.com/safari/aard/